PARACORD
jewelry

PARACORD

jewelry

35 stylish projects using traditional knotting techniques

Linda Peterson

CICO BOOKS
LONDON NEW YORK

This book is dedicated to the memory of my mother, Jane Molden, who lost her battle with breast cancer nearly three years ago. She was a tremendous role model, caregiver, and genuinely kind, warm, and loving person, who put her love of God and her family foremost in her life. She is someone I strive to be like every day so that I can do the same for my children and grandchildren. She will always continue to live on in my memory until, one day soon, we are reunited in Paradise.

Published in 2015 by CICO Books
An imprint of Ryland Peters & Small Ltd
20–21 Jockey's Fields   341 E 116th St
London WC1R 4BW   New York, NY 10029
www.rylandpeters.com

10 9 8 7 6 5 4 3 2 1

A CIP catalog record for this book is available from the Library of Congress and the British Library.

ISBN: 978 1 78249 192 7

Printed in China

Editor: **Marie Clayton**
Designer: **Mark Latter**
Step photographer: **Geoff Dann**
Style photographers: **Emma Mitchell**
and **Gavin Kingcome**
Stylist: **Luis Peral-Aranda**

In-house editor: **Carmel Edmonds**
In-house designer: **Fahema Khanam**
Art director: **Sally Powell**
Production controller: **David Hearn**
Publishing manager: **Penny Craig**
Publisher: **Cindy Richards**

CONTENTS

INTRODUCTION

As always, when I sit down to create, I tend to reflect on times gone by, some in the way distant past, and others not that long ago.

Flash back to 1973: I'm seven years old, just a little girl spending time shopping with Grandma at the local five and dime store in St. Louis, Missouri. It was a special "Grandma day" when she would take me there, just the two of us. They had bins and bins of tiny little toys for only a dime. My favorite bin was the one with the paratroopers. I would search to find just the right one—it had to be the one standing up because they would fly the best. Once I found it, I couldn't wait to get back to Grandma's house to play. I'd throw it up in the air and watch it gently fall to the ground only to wind the cord back up again, throw it and watch it fall all over again. Again and again, for hours and hours it provided me lots of cheap entertainment.

Another of my favorite pastimes was collecting little clover flowers in the yard. Grandma taught me that if you picked one and left a long enough stem, you could weave it into a ring and wear the flower. And so it came to be my first piece of woven jewelry. That was then…

Fast forward 40 years: a lot has changed, and while I'm no longer throwing toys up in the air or turning clover flowers into rings, I do find that my childhood memories come flashing back as I create my jewelry designs. It's what drives my passion to create and explore. I can't wait to have special Grandma days with my new granddaughter Carlee. I hope to pass these stories and creative talent on to her as she grows up, so she can keep it alive for future generations.

Creating jewelry with cords, yarns, floss, fibers, or even long stemmed clovers, is nothing new and knotting techniques and ideas have been around for years. What has changed, though, is the variety of materials available today. Years ago we didn't have access to a wide variety of colors or materials and we weren't as skilled at thinking outside the box, using materials intended for one purpose, but finding ways to re-invent them for another. Who would have thought of using the same cord that paratroopers use to create jewelry? A lot has changed for sure. Or maybe is it just that my imagination has gotten better? I don't know.

A lot of time I'm inspired by kids. I remember buying my children embroidery floss to make friendship bracelets.

These are still popular with kids because they're easy to create and the floss comes in a variety of colors. It's a great way to pass the time and the end result is creating bracelets to give as gifts or trade with friends. I used this inspiration as a springboard for the project on page 102, the Tri-strand Boho Bracelet.

Other projects that I have made serve both a fun and functional purpose. Perhaps you're a teacher or a sports coach—the Braided Lanyard (see page 90) is a fun project to make and useful to keep your identification and keys within reach. Or maybe you're a little daring and want to try your hand at creating a bigger project such as the Camouflage Belt (see page 86). With easy knotting techniques and a little time, you'll find these projects are very useful in your everyday life.

One special feature in this book is that I've devoted a whole chapter to "man crafts." Let's face it ladies, it's hard to create something for our guys! And guys, I know that there is not a whole lot of inspiration out there for you to work with. It's all girly stuff! So with that in mind, I designed some projects for the guys in our life and for you guys who want to create too! Keeping the colors organic and earthy always lends a masculine touch. These designs could easily be created with a favorite team color instead. Mix and match and just have fun. For the girly girls though, and those who want something with a little more frill, you'll love learning

some basic knots based on Asian culture. This style of knotting can take your paracord jewelry to a whole new level and turn the pieces into functional artwork that are quite decorative and feminine.

It amazes me how much the simplicity of some of these knots contrasts with the complexity that I see with my eyes. I think you too will be amazed when you dive into these projects and find that the process has a calming and soothing effect. I always feel better when I create! Many trendy designs can be made using very simple overhand or barrel knots only, so don't be afraid to keep it simple when starting out. As you get comfortable and familiar with the knots, I'm sure you will begin to have some favorites. Why not combine your favorite knots together in a new sequence to see what you discover? Or repeat your favorite knot over and over again to create a new design? Before you realize it, you'll be creating your very own patterns!

Just as with anything that is new, or if you're just beginning your creative journey, you are likely to make mistakes. Don't let that deter or discourage you. I make mistakes—I made mistakes with some of these designs. But generally these designs create a specific pattern that repeats, so if you keep an eye on your pattern, you will be able to quickly spot where you've gone wrong. Simply remove those stitches, and continue again; you don't always have to start back at the beginning. Think of mistakes as a good thing. I've made many happy discoveries that I might not have found otherwise, just because I made a mistake.

So I invite you to grab a tea—a big sweet tea in a mason jar for me, please—sit back, relax, knot away, and don't sweat the small stuff. Just remember to turn your flops into flopportunities!

Knot away!

Linda

chapter 1

TOOLS & TECHNIQUES

THE ART OF KNOTTING

Knotting techniques adopted from ancient Asian cultures have been around for centuries. They were originally functional and a part of everyday survival—ropes tied around the waist were secured with knots to hold essential tools, such as axes and hunting implements. Over time, however, knotting skills developed into more of an art form and began to be used as decorations on both clothing and home décor items.

Take a moment to search "decorative knots" on the Internet and you will find that it is indeed an art form! There are so many choices and possibilities and, to be quite honest, it can become very mind-boggling. In an effort to keep you sane—and myself as well—I have chosen knots for this book that, with just a few alterations, can give you many different looks. This means you can spend your time making beautiful jewelry, instead of learning hundreds of different knots and having nothing more than a bunch of beautiful knots to show for all your hard work. So please take a moment to familiarize yourself with this first section because it will serve as the basis for many of the projects that you will see in the book.

HOW MUCH CORD DO I NEED?

That is a million dollar question for sure! I wish I could give you an exact answer, but I can't. There are so many factors involved, such as the length of a necklace or bracelet, the diameter of the cord, just how tight you cinch the knots. Everyone has their own unique tension and everyone will create their knots slightly differently from the next person.

What I can tell you is that, when in doubt, add more cord. Depending on the size of the project you are working on, it can be an extra few inches/centimeters to an extra few feet/meters. I would much rather trim off a length of cord that I don't need than not have the length of cord that I do need. I have given an approximate length of cord for each project, but please bear in mind that these are only estimates and I encourage you to use your best judgment.

A HANDY FORMULA

When making a "bar" like the square macramé knot featured on page 27, or something like a braid, make a knot to create 1 in. (2.5 cm) of the finished length. Mark the cord with a piece of tape where it emerges at the beginning and the end of this finished sequence of knotting. Undo the cord and measure the length of cord needed to complete the 1 in. (2.5 cm) of bar or braid. You can then multiply this measurement by the actual finished length you need to make. For example, if it takes 5 in. (12.5 cm) of cord to create a 1 in. (2.5 cm) bar and you want your finished length to be 7 in. (17.5 cm), multiply 5 (12.5) by 7 to get 35 in. (87.5 cm) length of cord. Then I add on several inches/centimeters for good measure just to be sure.

MATERIALS AND TOOLS

It's always much easier—and more fun—to make things if you have the right materials and the correct tools. One of the best features of working with paracord is that you do not have to have a massive number of tools and the ones you do need are easy to source.

PARACORDS

Paracord is essentially parachute cord as used for many decades by the military, as well as those who enjoy outdoor sports, because of its ability to hold up under extreme weight. Typically it is classified by the amount of weight it will carry. However, over recent years paracord has gained popularity with many hobbyists. As a result, it is now available in a range of different colors, patterns, and weights for a variety of uses. I've used several thicknesses of paracord throughout this book. I like the way you can combine the size and color for different purposes. Paracord can be found at a number of online retailers as well as in major craft, hobby, and hardware stores.

Nano cord—1/33 in. (0.75 mm)

Micro cord—1/20 in. (1.18 mm)

275 tactical—3/32 in. (2.38 mm)

425—1/8 in. (3 mm)

550—3/16 in. (4.5 mm)

425 is substantially thicker than 275 at approximately ⅛ in. (3 mm) in diameter. I like the look and feel of this when I want to create a thicker bar, such as in the Men's Watch on page 80, or when I want to create a more masculine feel to a project.

550 is the most commonly known cord and can be found in many hardware stores. It is approximately ³⁄₁₆ in. (4.5 mm) in diameter. Use this if you want to create a survival bracelet or you want a more bulky masculine feel to your design. It is very durable.

These cords generally come in a hank.

Nano cord is the thinnest paracord available—it's approximately ⅓₃ in. (0.75 mm) thick. It is very, very delicate and will give an almost lacy effect to your jewelry.

Micro cord is also a thin paracord—it's approximately ⅟₂₀ in. (1.18 mm) thick. Slightly heavier than the nano cord, I like to use this especially for barrel knots and for designs where I want a light look and feel.

Both nano and micro cords generally come on a spool.

275 tactical cord is among my favorites to work with, because the size of the cord gives your design a little bit of weight without making it too bulky or looking too masculine. It is approximately ³⁄₃₂ in. (2.38 mm) thick. The 275 stands for the amount of weight in pounds it will hold.

CLASPS AND CLIPS

There are many different clasps and fasteners available so you can choose something to suit your project. Though I've not used all the fasteners shown here, these are ones that are the most common.

Top row: swivel trigger clasps, screw D-rings. *Bottom row*: plastic clip fasteners in assorted sizes, colors, and types.

FINDINGS, BEADS, AND WIRES

A finding is the term used to describe all the small components that are used to join, fasten, or assemble jewelry pieces.

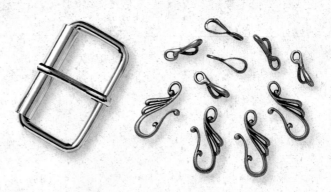

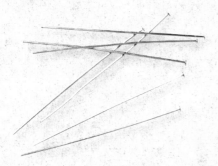

Hook-and-eye fasteners and belt buckles are available in a range of sizes and designs.

Head pins can be used to make dangles (see page 22).

Thousands of **beads** and **spacer beads** are available online and at many craft stores— here is a very small selection of them.

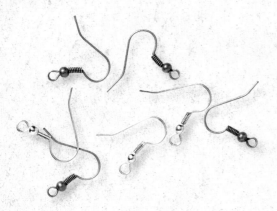

Earring wires are ideal to make hanging earrings.

Wooden beads of various types, as well as semi-precious stones in a range of shapes and sizes, work well with the more earthy colors of paracord. Silver spinners add a bit of movement and sparkle and I pick these up in bulk at my local sporting goods store in the fishing department.

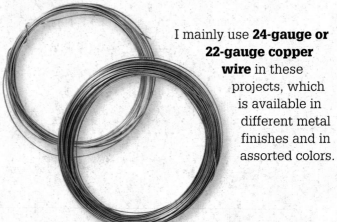

I mainly use **24-gauge or 22-gauge copper wire** in these projects, which is available in different metal finishes and in assorted colors.

Jump rings come in many sizes and different colors—they are used to add on or join components.

Rhinestone cup chain (left) can be used to add some sparkle, while heavier chain (top) is ideal for chunky key chains. Large hole spacer beads (bottom left) can be fairly plain or quite decorative and lend a nice touch. Look for more unusual bits to use—washers, metal nuts, and plastic rings (above center) can be ideal substitutes for beads and decorative rings (center right). Cord ends (bottom right) can be used to add a clasp (below center) to cords or ribbon.

Conchos (top row) are purely decorative pieces that are attached with a small screw from the reverse. They come in many different sizes, designs, and colors and add some nice accent to otherwise plain cords. D-rings (bottom right) are used at the end of belts and straps—you can fold the end of a strap over the flat bar of the D-ring and then use it as a base to attach the strap. Split rings are also useful as decoration when attaching handles to purses/handbags and for making key fobs.

TOOLS

These tools are the ones that I find the most useful.

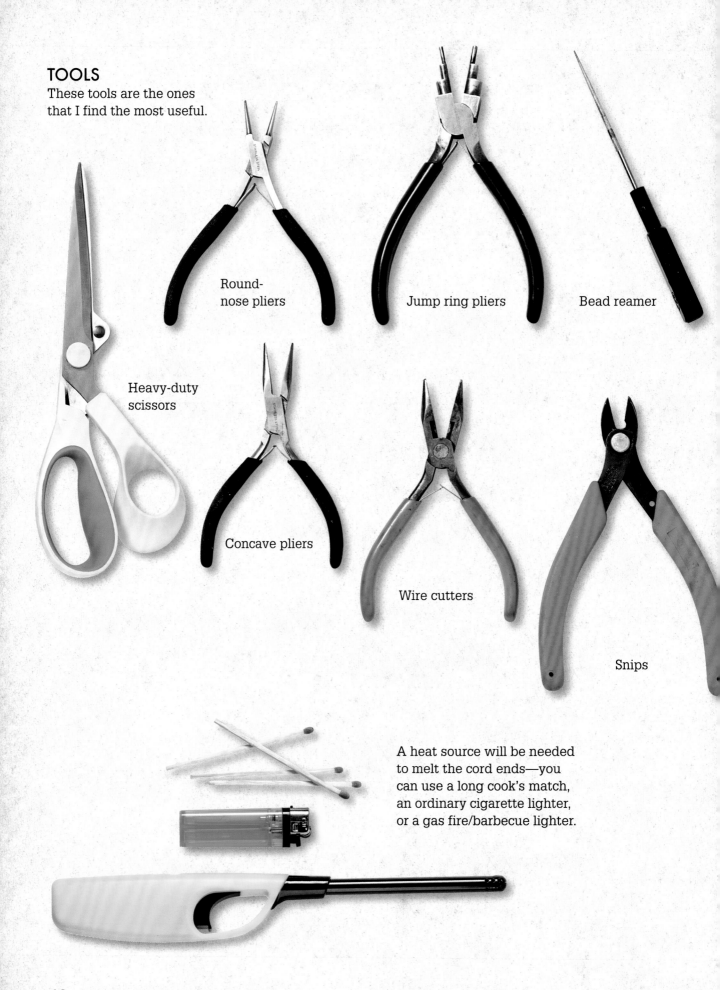

Round-nose pliers

Jump ring pliers

Bead reamer

Heavy-duty scissors

Concave pliers

Wire cutters

Snips

A heat source will be needed to melt the cord ends—you can use a long cook's match, an ordinary cigarette lighter, or a gas fire/barbecue lighter.

Clips are useful to hold cords in place as you work.

The bench block is used with the hammer when hammering in eyelets or snaps.

A lacing or fid needle (left) is used for weaving cords. Needles with large eyes (right) are used for threading and sewing.

ADHESIVES

There are many different types of adhesives and it's important to choose the correct one for the material and the project. Silicone-based adhesive is used for most of the projects where you need to attach an embellishment. Fabric and tacky glue are useful to add extra strength to finished ends so that they don't unwind.

TECHNIQUES

This is a special section in the book that you will refer to often. I use this section to outline the basic steps needed that are repeated in several projects throughout the book; a cross reference in the project will bring you to the correct page in the techniques section. Any special techniques or instructions that are specific to a particular project are detailed within that project.

SINGEING THE END OF THE CORD

Because paracord is made up of lots of smaller cords, the ends tend to unravel and fray. To prevent this, immediately singe to seal off the ends as described below.

1. Hold the cut end next to the flame of a lighter or match for a couple of seconds until the end begins to melt. It isn't necessary to hold the end in the flame.

2. Allow to cool slightly, but while it is still tacky roll the end between your fingers to seal all the ends and prevent them from fraying. But be careful! It can get hot.

HELPFUL HINTS

You can use a gas barbecue or fire lighter instead of a lighter, or a long cook's match.

The melted cord will be hot at first—make sure it's cooled enough to touch before rolling with your fingers. I dip my fingers into cold water before I seal the ends—this prevents me from burning my fingers. Be careful because if the ends are too hot the plastic will stick to your fingers and not peel off.

To stop the braid or knots from unraveling, I tuck the cord end(s) under another strand on the reverse while the ends are still soft and melted from the lighter. If the ends will show, I use a dab of fabric or tacky glue to secure the end instead. Sometimes I do both. When in doubt, glue!

ADDING A LACING NEEDLE

A lacing needle, also called a fid, is particularly helpful when you are weaving long cords such as the cords in the Cell Phone Pouch on page 118. It's also helpful to tuck the ends of cords back into the pattern as you will see on page 65. Slightly heat the end and twist the needle on. As the end cools it will grab the threads inside the fid. Simply twist in the opposite direction to remove the needle.

OPENING AND CLOSING JUMP RINGS

Use this simple method to open and close jump rings so you can use them to attach clasps or join components together.

1 To open the jump ring, hold a pair of pliers on each side of the join and twist the pliers slightly in opposite directions to open up a gap.

2 To close the ring, repeat the twisting action in reverse to bring the two ends back together neatly.

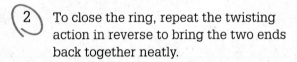

HELPFUL HINT

It's not a good idea to open a jump ring by pulling the ends apart—this will distort the shape and it will be hard to get it back into a perfect circle. Open them as shown here and they will stay perfectly round.

CREATING A BEADED DANGLE

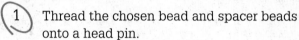 Thread the chosen bead and spacer beads onto a head pin.

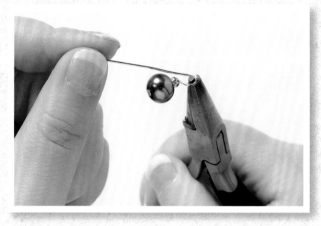

② Use round-nose pliers to curve the top of the head pin into a loop, centering the loop over the beads. Cut off the excess head pin.

③ For a more decorative dangle, just thread on a selection of beads—you can use different shapes and colors.

WRAPPING

A simple technique to change the look of a cord or add extra dimension or color quickly. This can also be used to attach something to the cord. It's a great technique if you want to make a piece of jewelry in a matter of minutes or to use up small bits of cord.

Use nano cord to secure decorative chain to a length of cord by wrapping around.

Take one of the thicker cords and wrap it with a micro or nano cord in a contrasting color.

KNOTTING TECHNIQUES

These knots are the ones used most frequently in the projects, sometimes with variations that are detailed within the project itself.

DEFINITIONS

Although I try not to use technical terms, it will help if you understand some of the terminology used in the book.

Bight: A line curved into a U shape. It does not form a completed loop.

Running end: The end that you are threading or weaving.

Stationary end: A strand that remains where it is and is not used to weave—rather it generally has other strands knotted or woven around it.

Loop: A cord that crosses over itself and forms a circle.

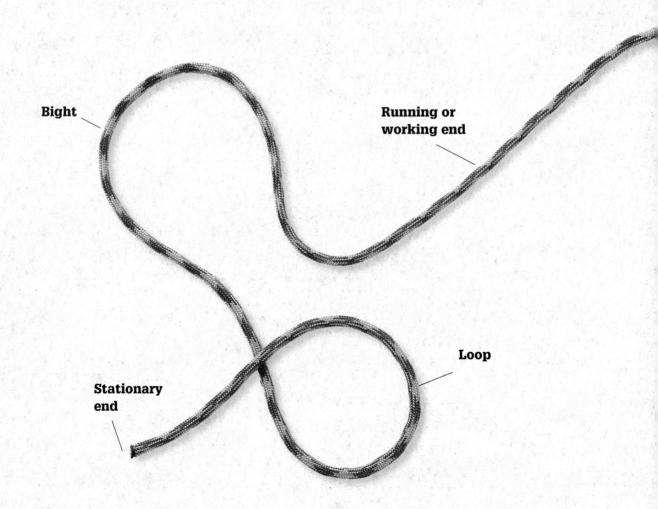

Bight

Running or working end

Loop

Stationary end

LARK'S HEAD KNOT

A useful knot for attaching and anchoring a loop of cord to a ring or a finding before you begin the design. It's also known as a cow hitch. This is one knot I use frequently when working with basic macramé techniques.

1 Fold the cord or cords in half and feed the loop through the finding.

2 Bring all the cord ends down and through the loop and pull to tighten.

BARREL KNOT

For me, learning this knot changed everything when it came to making knotted jewelry. It's one of the simplest knots to create and yet the strength of this knot is nearly unbeatable. It not only lends a beautiful finish to your jewelry pieces, it can be used in numerous decorative ways as well. For most projects you'll need a minimum length of 10–12 in. (25–30 cm). If you want a wider knot, just add additional length.

1 Hold the end of the cord and wrap it around the center base cords three to four times with your right hand.

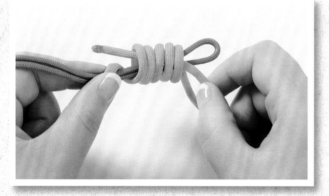

2 Thread the right end of the cord through the middle of the knot and out again at the left side.

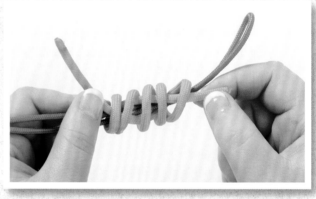

3 Thread the left end of the cord through the middle of the knot and out again at the right side.

4 Gently pull on both cord ends to tighten the knot, making sure the barrel knot is positioned tightly against the clasp or the knotted end.

5 To seal the final ends, trim off excess cord leaving about ⅛ in. (3 mm). Bend the center cords back away from the flame and carefully seal the trimmed cord with a flame as explained on page 20.

SQUARE KNOT

This is one of the basic macramé knots, also known as a Solomon's knot. This knot creates a bar that is often used in making bracelets. The center cords are much shorter than the outer cords since they remain in the same place. You will have two sets of cords; a center set and an outer set. I always begin this knot by working with the right side first.

I find it helpful to anchor the top of this bar to the table with a piece of tape to prevent it from slipping. It makes it much easier to pull up on the cords as you are working.

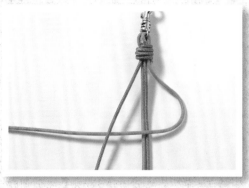

1) Anchor the cords to your finding. Take the right outer strand over the center strands and under the left outer strand.

2) Take the left outer strand under the center strands, up through the loop and over the right outer strand.

3) Pull gently on the cord ends to tighten the first half of the square knot.

4) Take the left outer strand over the center strands and under the right outer strand.

5) Take the right outer strand under the center strands, up through the loop and over the left outer strand.

6) Pull gently on the cord ends to tighten the completed square knot.

HELPFUL HINT

To estimate the length of cords required for this knot, measure the finished length you need, add 4 in. (10 cm), and multiply by two. Cut one cord to this measurement—this will become the inner cord. For the outside cord, take the finished length you need, multiply by eight, and cut the outer cord to this dimension.

BRAID (PLAIT)

To create visual interest, I often mix and match my knots and braids together to create unique compositions. You can also braid with multiple colors as well as cords of different thicknesses to create a unique look.

HELPFUL HINT

To keep the braid straight and even as you work, hook the loop or ring onto something to secure it, so you are braiding under tension.

BASIC BRAID WITH ONE OR MORE CORDS IN A GROUP

1 Cut three strands of cord following the 1 in. (2.5 cm) formula found on page 13. Fold each cord in half and bring the loops together. Grasp the cords with your fingers and secure them according to the project directions.

2 Alternatively you can attach the cords to a ring or clasp with a lark's head knot (see page 25). Making one lark's head knot with all three looped strands can be bulky—if you want to avoid this, knot each cord loop onto the ring separately.

3 Separate the cords into three sections with two strands each. Bring the group on the right over the center.

4 Next, bring the left-hand strands over and into the center.

5 Continue to repeat steps 3 and 4 until the braid is the desired length.

6 Tighten the cords as you go for a neat and even braid. Finish the braid as given in the project.

FOUR-STRAND BRAID VARIATION

This is also a braiding technique, but using four strands instead of three.

1. Fold two cords in half and attach to the appropriate finding according to the project instructions. Criss-cross the two center strands with the left over the right. You will now have two strands toward the left and two toward the right.

2. Bring the outer left-hand strand under the next strand to the right and then off toward the right. You should now have three strands pointing to the right and one strand to the left.

3. Take the outer right strand, cross it over the next strand to the left and under the following strand. Make sure that your braid resembles that shown in the picture.

4. Take the outer right strand over the next strand to the left, and then take the outer left strand under and over the next two strands to the right. Repeat the sequence in this step until you have the desired length.

HELPFUL HINT

Essentially you are weaving a strand over one cord and under the next and then reversing the sequence so that the following or opposite group is then under and over. This locks the braided cords into place. I braid a little at a time and then check my pattern. If I find that I've made a mistake, I can easily go back and correct it.

SIX-STRAND BRAID VARIATION

Another variation on the braiding technique—using six strands instead of three creates a wider, more masculine band. Here six individual strands are braided to create a watch strap.

1. Attach the three strands to one side of the watch with a lark's head knot (see page 25). Criss-cross the center two strands, with the left strand over the right.

2. Take the outermost right strand and, working toward the left, cross it under then over and stop. Take the outermost left strand, working toward the right and cross it over, under, over.

3. Take the outermost right strand and cross under, over, stop. Take the outermost left strand and cross over, under, over.

4. Continue repeating step 3 until you have the desired length.

OVERHAND KNOT

This knot is probably the simplest knot there is to make. We use it quite often in everyday life and probably don't even realize it. I use this knot as a decorative element, but also as a slip knot.

1. Thread one end over the other and round through the loop.

2. When the knot is made over one or more threads it can slide along, which is useful if you want to make a necklace or bracelet that is adjustable in length.

BLANKET KNOT

Similar to blanket stitch in sewing, this is a variation of the half hitch knot. It's useful to cover rings and straps.

1. To start making the knot, create a bight on top of the ring with the running end of the cord down through the center of the ring. The most important thing to remember is always to loop and come through in the same direction to create an even pattern. Check the pattern often.

2. Take the running end of the cord back up through the cord loop. Tighten the knot to the right. Repeat until the ring is completely covered. Trim ends and singe (see page 20). Tuck the end under one of the strands to conceal it.

POPCORN KNOT

I am particularly fond of this knot because it has so many variations. Again, don't let the number of steps fool you into thinking this is complicated—once you have the hang of this knot you will see that you can complete a ball in just a matter of a minute or so! This knot makes a cute popcorn-like ball; it is also known as a Turk's head, a button knot, or a paracord ball.

1　Begin by wrapping the cord around a bar or finger to create an X shape.

2　Bring the running end up over the center of the X, and then take it under the right strand and out the side.

3　Rotate the knot slightly toward you. Take the left-hand loop over the right-hand loop to make a new X.

4　Take the running end on the right over the right loop, through the center, under the left loop and out the side.

5　Rotate the knot slightly toward you again and place the right loop over the left loop to form a new X.

6　Take the running end on the left over the left loop, through the center and under the right loop, coming out the side. Notice that you have two ends that are now parallel to each other.

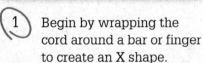

7 Slide the knot off the rod and place it on your index finger. Gently cinch the threads, each section at a time, to tighten and decrease the size of the knot. It will begin to form a curved ball.

8 Continue to build the ball by threading the right working end through the loop, following the exact pattern you just created.

9 As you continue following the pattern previously set, each line becomes a double strand. You will see the shape of the popcorn ball build symmetrically.

10 This shows the completed popcorn knot. Trim and singe the ends (see page 20) as suggested in the project instructions.

ROSETTE KNOT

Once you have mastered the popcorn ball, this knot will be super simple as it is the exact same knot just made flat to create a rosette. It is also known as a flat button knot.

1. Begin by wrapping the cord around a bar to create an X shape.

2. Bring the running end up over the center of the X, and then take it under the right strand and out the side.

3. Rotate the knot slightly toward you. Take the left-hand loop over the right-hand loop to make a new X.

4. The right running end comes over the right loop, through the center and out the left bar.

5. Rotate the knot slightly toward you. Take the right-hand loop over the left-hand loop to make a new X.

6. Take the running end on the left over the left loop, through the center and under the right loop coming out the side. Notice that you have two ends that are now parallel to each other.

(7) Slip the knot off the rod, open up and flatten into a flower shape. Notice the two parallel cords in the upper center.

(8) Continue the exact same pattern as set. Take the right running end, create a bight, and thread it through the loops using the previous lines of cord as a guide. As you continue each line becomes a double strand.

(9) Eventually you will have this finished rosette shape. Trim and singe the ends as instructed in the project.

CELTIC KNOT

I like this knot because you don't have to secure it to a finding and the ends have a clean finished look to them, which makes it nice for making bracelets and choker-style necklaces. The Celtic knot creates an attractive woven effect.

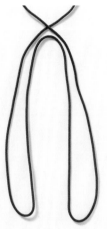 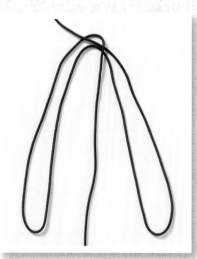 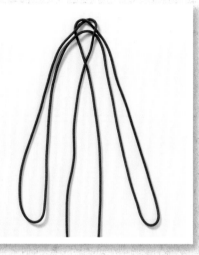

1. Find the center of the cord and fold each end upward creating a bight on each side that is the measurement of the desired finished length. My finished bracelet is 6 in. (15 cm) long so each side loop measures 6 in. (15 cm). Cross the right end over the left end at the top.

2. Bend the right running end down over the two right strands.

3. Bend the left running end back under the two left strands and over the right running end.

4. Take the right single middle strand and place it under the two strands on the right.

5. Take the left single middle strand and lay it over the top of the two strands on the left. Cross the double left strands over the double right strands. Repeat from step 2 to form the pattern.

CHINESE LOVE KNOT

This pretty decorative knot is also known as the double coin knot, a decorative knot that some say has the look of two Chinese coins overlapping. I call it a Chinese Love Knot because for me it's a symbol of everlasting love despite all the twists and turns in life.

① Cut the appropriate length of two cords and find the center. Hold the cords so that the curve or bight is at the top. Take the right pair of running ends over the left strands, up and around over the bight, creating two loops as shown. It should look like a pretzel.

② Take the same pair of running ends under the bottom pair of strands and round to the left.

③ Thread the running ends over the left loop, under the first pair of strands in the middle, over the next pair of strands in the middle and out under the right loop.

LEAF KNOT

I really like how this simple knot creates a leaf shape and this is why I call it the leaf knot. It's also known as the pipa knot.

1. Working from top down, create a bight and then wrap the running end around the stationary end at the top as shown in the picture.

2. Create another bight in the center of the previous loop and wrap the running end around the top again. Repeat this step a third time, with each loop making the hole in the center smaller.

3. To finish, tuck the working end through the middle of the lower loop to secure. Tighten if necessary, trim, and singe the ends (see page 20).

ROYAL CROWN SINNET

Despite the number of steps, this is not a complicated knot—it is much easier than it looks. When completed it creates a nice, round, tubular rope. What I love about this knot is that when you use two different cord colors together you get a spiraling effect.

 1 Wind the first color twice around your finger.

2 Slide the second color through both loops on your finger.

3 Take the right end of the second cord and loop it back over the top, down through the center, under the remaining cord, and out at the other side.

 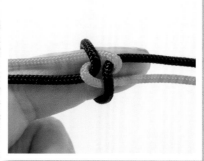 

4 Take the left end of the same cord, and loop it back over the top, down through the center, under the remaining cord, and out the other side.

5 Cinch the knot to tighten it and adjust to create a square form. This is the basic square structure of the knot.

6 Separate the strands as shown in the picture. One color should be side to side and the other color up and down.

 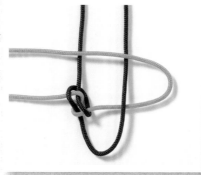 

7 Take the bottom strand, form a bight upward, and lay it over the strand on the right side.

8 Take the right strand, form a bight, and lay it over the next two strands.

9 Take the left upward pointing strand, form a bight, and lay it over the two strands pointing to the left.

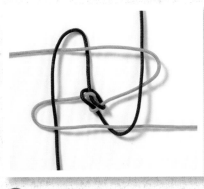

10 Take the bottom strand facing left, form a bight, and lay it over the next two strands, through the center of the first loop and under, coming out the right side.

11 Slide a finger into the initial loop again and pull on the strands gently to tighten the cords into the square. This will tighten the knot and leave a loop at the base to be used later as a clasp.

12 Continue the pattern by repeating steps 7 to 11 to create the length of rounded cord needed for the project. Every so often check your pattern to make sure it is spiraling neatly.

HELPFUL HINT
You might find it easier to rotate the knot each time as you take the cords in a counterclockwise direction, so you are always working in the same orientation.

chapter 2

KNOTTY DESIGNS

PINK *popcorn*

I just love the playfulness of this bracelet with its "pop" of bright and cheerful colors! It's such a fun and easy bracelet to make in a short amount of time, so why not make several to match the colors of your wardrobe?

MATERIALS

5 approx. 18 in. (45 cm) lengths of 550 paracord in light pink

5 approx. 18 in. (45 cm) lengths of 550 paracord in dark pink

Scissors

Lighter

Pliers

Large eye needle

Stretch cord

20 silver spacer beads

10 crystal beads

1. Make five light pink and five dark pink popcorn balls following the instructions on page 32. Trim and singe the ends. To hide the ends, push them into the inside of the ball using the tip of a pair of pliers.

2. Thread the stretch cord through a needle. Thread the popcorn balls alternately onto the stretch cord, adding a silver spacer, crystal bead, silver spacer between each pair.

3. Knot the stretch cord and then tuck the knot inside the nearest ball so it is hidden.

HELPFUL HINT

Using 550 cord makes quite large popcorns; for a smaller ball use thinner cord. You can also make matching earrings using thinner cording.

BLUE *bayou*

The colors of this necklace remind me of the calming colors of the sea and the soothing sound of the ocean waves. In this design we are not only creating the necklace but also using a blanket stitch to make our own focal pendant.

MATERIALS

Approx. 36 in. (90 cm) of 275 tactical paracord in turquoise

2 approx. 36 in. (90cm) lengths of 275 tactical paracord in pacific blue

3 approx. 36 in. (90 cm) lengths of nano paracord in white

3 approx. 36 in. (90 cm) lengths of nano paracord in dark blue

2 approx. 36 in. (90 cm) lengths of nano paracord in light blue

Scissors

Lighter

2 head pins

2 cone-shaped bead caps

Round-nose pliers

Wire cutters

Plastic ring, approx. 1 in. (2.5 cm) in diameter

Approx. 26 in. (66 cm) of 275 tactical paracord in turquoise

5 assorted cord-wrapped rings

Jump rings

Lobster or toggle clasp

1. Holding all the strands together, tie an overhand knot about ¼ in. (5 mm) from the end (see page 31). Separate the strands into two sections. Loop the right section over the left strands, around the back side, under the strands, and up through the loop.

2. Leave a gap of about 4 in. (10 cm) and then loop the left section over the right, around the back side, under the strands, and up through the loop. Repeat left and right knots another four times, leaving a space between each, and a 4-in. (10-cm) gap before the final overhand knot. Trim and singe the cord ends just after the final knot (see page 20).

3. Thread a head pin through one of the end knots so the head of the pin catches securely in one of the cords.

4 Thread the cone-shaped bead cap onto the head pin and over the ends to conceal.

5 Create a loop at the end of the head pin with a pair of round-nose pliers and trim off excess wire. Repeat this step for the opposite side.

6 Cover the plastic ring with turquoise paracord using blanket knots (see page 31). Thread all the rings onto the necklace. Attach a toggle clasp with jump rings to the ends.

HELPFUL HINTS

If you don't want to purchase cord-wrapped rings or you can't find the colors you need, simply wrap your own blank rings in the colors of your choice using the blanket knot technique.

Add as many different rings as you like.

NIGHT *at the disco*

When I was designing this necklace I knew I wanted something bright and flashy with a sense of FUN! The fluorescent cords really glow under disco lights, so this necklace makes quite a statement on a night out.

1 Create your own multicolored strands by wrapping the 275 orange cords with pink nano cords.

MATERIALS

2 approx. 42 in. (107 cm) lengths of 275 tactical paracord in orange

4 approx. 42 in. (107 cm) lengths of nano paracord in dark pink

2 approx. 42 in. (107 cm) lengths of 275 tactical paracord in turquoise

2 approx. 42 in. (107 cm) lengths of 550 paracord in bright pink

2 approx. 42 in. (107 cm) lengths of micro paracord in green

Scissors

Lighter

2 Gather your cords, except the green micro paracord, together in your hand. Make sure you have a variety of cord thicknesses and colors along with some wrapped cords.

3 Make an overhand knot (see page 31) in the center and two more spaced around 4 in. (10 cm) on either side. Adjust the knot if necessary so it forms a pretty V shape.

4. Using a contrast color (green) of micro cord, make a barrel knot (see page 26) on either side of each overhand knot to add a little decoration and to prevent the knot from slipping.

5. To create the fastening, tie an overhand knot on one end. Trim and singe the ends (see page 20). Make a loop on one end and secure with a barrel knot—make sure that your loop is large enough to fit over the knot on the opposite end but not too large for it not to hold.

HELPFUL HINT

This is a great project to use up leftover lengths and thicknesses of cord. There is no wrong way to create this necklace—have fun playing with unique color combinations.

BLUE DANGLE
earrings

Create these delicate earrings with nano paracord and accent each with a small pearl dangle to catch a sparkle of light.

1 Put one strand of each color together and make a Chinese love knot as explained on page 37. Make an overhand knot at the top and then trim the ends close to the knot and singe (see page 20).

MATERIALS

2 approx. 15 in. (38 cm) lengths of nano paracord in light blue

2 approx. 15 in. (38 cm) lengths of nano paracord in dark blue

Scissors

Lighter

2 jump rings

2 earring wires

Pliers

2 small pearl beads

2 head pins

2 Thread a jump ring through the knot at the top of the earring and attach an earring wire to the jump ring before closing it.

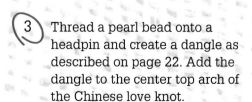

3 Thread a pearl bead onto a headpin and create a dangle as described on page 22. Add the dangle to the center top arch of the Chinese love knot.

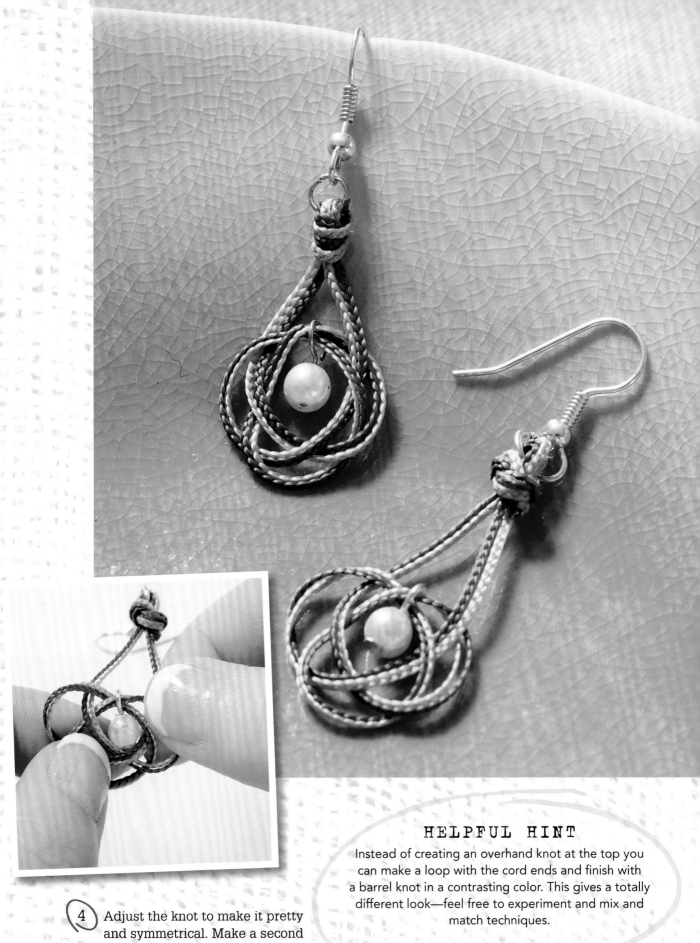

HELPFUL HINT

Instead of creating an overhand knot at the top you can make a loop with the cord ends and finish with a barrel knot in a contrasting color. This gives a totally different look—feel free to experiment and mix and match techniques.

4 Adjust the knot to make it pretty and symmetrical. Make a second earring the same way.

RISING *star*

A simple knotting technique creates a basic bracelet with a variety of looks, depending on the finding you choose.

① Use the longer length of cord to cover the plastic ring in blanket knots (see page 31). Find the center of one shorter length and make an overhand knot (see page 31). Leaving a gap of about 1 in. (2.5 cm), take the left running end under the other, back over the top, and down through the loop.

② Bring the running end around to the front and then up through the loop that has been formed to the right.

MATERIALS

Approx. 18 in. (45 cm) of 550 paracord in brown

Plastic ring

2 approx. 8 in. (20 cm) lengths of 550 paracord in brown

Scissors

Lighter

Additional lengths of 550 paracord in brown

Approx. 8–12 in. (20–30 cm) of micro paracord in brown

Triangular green bead and rhinestone finding

E6000 silicone-based glue

HELPFUL HINT

Adjust the length of the bracelet by taking away or adding some length to the loops on each side. The lengths given are approximate and will vary due to individual wrist sizes and tightness of the knots.

3 Pull the knot tight to complete. You should have a loop at the top and the bottom with a knot in the middle. Trim off excess cord, leaving ends of around ¼ in. (5 mm), and singe the ends to finish. Use the second shorter length to make a second side piece the same way.

4 Thread the end of a separate short length of cord through the loop end of one side piece to form an overhand knot, but before pulling tight put one end through the middle of the loop. Pull tight to create a toggle loop at the end.

5 Use additional cord to make a popcorn ball (see page 32) and tie this over the overhand knot at the end of the second side piece as a toggle. Singe the ends. Attach the bottom loop of each side piece to the covered ring with a barrel knot (see page 26) using the brown micro cord. Glue the finding over the center ring.

CHINESE KNOT *necklace*

Create some Oriental style with this pretty necklace based on a Chinese love knot. Make a coordinating pair of earrings following the instructions on page 50.

following the instructions on page 50.

MATERIALS

2 approx. 50 in. (125 cm) lengths of 550 paracord in green

Scissors

Lighter

1 Make a Chinese love knot (see page 37). At one top corner, thread both ends over and through the loop, bringing one strand out on each side of the doubled strand. Repeat on the other side to hold the knot in its shape.

2 Make an overhand knot (see page 31) on one pair of strands, just above the Chinese love knot. Carefully pull tight. Repeat on the other side.

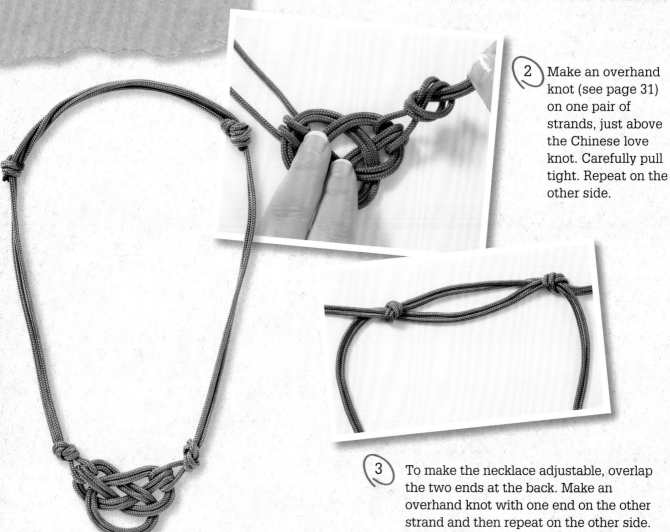

3 To make the necklace adjustable, overlap the two ends at the back. Make an overhand knot with one end on the other strand and then repeat on the other side. Trim the cord ends close to each knot and singe to seal (see page 20).

PURPLE *passion*

Using nano cord gives this necklace a delicate, lacy look. Although it looks amazingly complex, it uses only simple square knots—just make sure you know exactly which strands you need to work with on a particular step. We will be working with one side of the necklace at a time.

1. Fold all the cords in half and bind with a barrel knot (see page 26) to make a loop. Divide the cords into two groups of eight.

2. Working on one set of eight cords only and using a pair of cords as each strand, make two square knots (see page 27) and pull tight. Leave a small gap and make another complete square knot. Leave another small gap and make a third complete square knot. Still working on the same side, divide the eight cords into two sets of four strands. Make two complete square knots on one set of four strands. Pull the cords tight then repeat with the other set of four strands.

3. Leaving a gap, take the center four strands (the two inner strands from each set) and make two square knots). Leave another gap and repeat twice more, again leaving a gap in between the square knots.

MATERIALS

8 approx. 42 in. (105 cm) lengths of nano paracord in purple

Scissors

Lighter

Beaded dangle

Jump ring

Pliers

4 Divide the eight cords into two sets of four strands as in step 2. Leave a gap and make a square knot on each set of these four strands.

5 Working with all 8 cords and using a pair of cords as each strand, create a square knot. Leave a large gap, work two more square knots, leave a gap, and make an overhand knot. Trim and singe the ends (see page 20). This completes one side of the necklace.

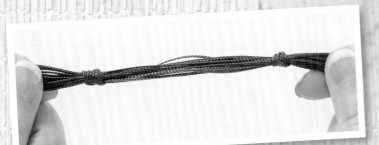

6 Make the second side of the necklace in the same way. Overlap the two sets of ends at the back. Make an overhand knot with one set of ends on the other group of strands and then repeat on the other side— the knots will slide for an adjustable necklace. Add a dangle at the front using a jump ring.

HELPFUL HINT

Work one complete side of the necklace first so that you have it as a guide to follow for the other half.

BLUE *moon*

This elegant bracelet with its discreet flash of rhinestones reminds me of stars in a night sky. Wear it with an evening outfit or just to brighten your day.

MATERIALS

Approx. 48 in. (120 cm) of 275 tactical paracord in dark blue

6 European-style large hole silver spacer beads

2 rhinestone European-style large hole spacer beads

Approx. 10 in. (25 cm) of 275 tactical paracord in dark blue

Scissors

Lighter

Toggle clasp

1 Using the longer cord, make the first sequence of a Celtic knot (see page 36).

2 Slide a silver spacer bead onto the two single strands in the center and up to the base of the knot. Leave the design fairly loose so you can see the pattern emerging.

HELPFUL HINT

I like to use European-style beads for this project because the larger hole in the center will fit over thicker cords when other beads will not. This allows me to add a little extra design element and interest to my jewelry designs.

3 To secure the bead, continue the knotting sequence, and then add another silver spacer bead. Continue knotting and then at the center of your bracelet add a spacer bead, rhinestone bead, and spacer bead. Repeat the sequence of knotting and adding spacer beads.

4 At the end you will have two
loops and two single strand
ends. Place the loops together
and thread the right running
end through the loop.

5 String a final rhinestone bead
the same cord and take it back
through the two loops. Fasten
the end in place by making a
barrel knot (see page 26) with
the separate length of cord.
Trim off the excess cord and
singe (see page 20). Add a
toggle clasp to the other end
of the bracelet.

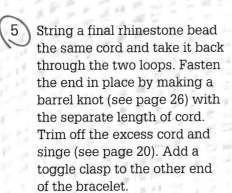

EVERLASTING *love*

Sometimes you can create your own unique knots by starting with one pattern and altering it in the middle of the sequence. This take on the Celtic knot does just that. It creates an open knot with pretty dangles, making a delicate and attractive necklace.

1 Find the centers and criss-cross two cords, with one angled from top left to bottom right and the other from top right to bottom left.
The running end off to the right side should go over and under the other cord and the running end off to the left should go under and over.
Add a third cord running horizontally across the top, over both left-hand strands, under the first right strand and over the second right strand as shown in the picture.

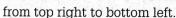

MATERIALS

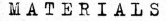

3 approx. 42–48 in. (105–120 cm) lengths of 275 tactical paracord in brown

Beaded dangles

Jump ring

Pliers

Scissors

Lighter

2 Criss-cross the two single strands in the center with the left over the top of the right.

3 Take the double right running ends over the right single strand. Take the double left running ends under the left single strand and criss-cross them over the other double strands in the center.

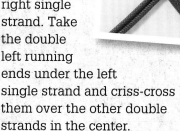

HELPFUL HINT

This necklace ended up taking more cord that I had originally allowed so I ended up with ends that were too short to complete the necklace. I lengthened the cords by splicing a new cord onto the old one, by melting each end and pressing them together until they cooled. I concealed the join with a decorative barrel knot.

4 Take the two single strands around, taking the right strand over the double strands on the right and the left strand under the double strands on the left, to meet in the center.

5 Take the double running ends on the left under the two center strands and over the right double strands.

6 Bring the same running ends around over the strands in the center and through the loop on the left as shown in the picture.

7 Continue bringing the same running ends back to meet all the other strands. Secure with a barrel knot. Add dangles of your choice and fasten at the back as described in step 6 of Purple Passion on page 57.

MATERIALS

Approx. 18 in. (45 cm) of 550 paracord in brown

Scissors

Lighter

Large eye embroidery needle

Short length of nano paracord in green

Approx. 18 in. (45 cm) of 550 paracord in pink

E6000 silicone-based adhesive

Headband

ROSE *headband*

Headbands are coming back into fashion. Dress up an ordinary headband with a bouquet of flowers and add a little embroidery for accent.

1   Use the brown paracord to make the leaf. Loop the cord into a figure 8 shape with a larger loop at the bottom and a smaller loop at the top. The smaller loop is wrapped around the back of the stationery end as shown in the photo.

2   Use the working end to create a loop in the center of the previous loop and wrap around the neck again. Continue this pattern, fitting the bottom loop inside the previous loop each time and wrapping the top loop round the back at the top.

3   Tuck the working end through the middle of the lower loop to secure; trim and singe.

4   Thread the needle with green nano paracord and stitch the veins onto the front of the leaf.

5   Make four rosettes (see page 34) in pink cord, two large and two small. Shape them all into a cup with your fingers. Glue the smaller into the larger.

6   Glue the leaves and rosettes onto the headband, using the photograph as a guide.

HELPFUL HINT

I wrapped my headband in ribbon for a more coordinated look, but this is optional—there are so many different types of headbands available that you will probably be able to find something suitable ready-made. You can also attach these decorations to a hair tie or a barrette.

HELPFUL HINTS

To work out the amount of cord you need, measure the flip-flop strap from center front to where it goes through the sole. For each 1 in. (2.5 cm) you will need 11 in. (27.5 cm) plus another 4 in. (10 cm) of cord. Double this measurement for the length of cord for each shoe.

For more bling, add a cabochon or a brooch over the join in the straps at the front. Or consider using pretty ribbon for the knotting for a more delicate look.

HITCH KNOT *flip-flops*

Give ordinary plastic flip-flops some designer chic by creating knotted straps. The knot used here is a simple half hitch.

1 Measure the straps from one side to the other and then see page 64 for how much cord to cut. Loop the cord around the strap with one end to one side of the toe post.

see page 64

MATERIALS

Pair of plastic flip-flops

550 paracord (for measurement see tip box)

Scissors

Lacing needle

Lighter

2 Using the right running end, create a bight on top of the plastic strap. Thread the running end under and around the plastic strap and back up through the loop. Pull tight.

3 Keep repeating step 2 along the strap to the end, until no more of the plastic strap shows. Cut the excess cord, leaving a 3 in. (7.5 cm) tail. Thread the cord onto a lacing needle if desired and thread the tail back through the last few knots.

4 Bring the end out through one of the knots, trim off excess cord and singe. Repeat steps 2 and 3 along the other strap. Repeat all steps for the second flip-flop.

CELL PHONE *cable*

If your house is anything like ours, your cell phone cables inconveniently get "borrowed." Cover your cable so you know which is whose—it will also protect the cable from minor damage.

MATERIALS

Cell phone cable	Scissors
Tape measure	Lighter
550 paracord in pink (for measurement see tip box)	Micro paracord in neon green (for measurement see tip box)

1 Using the pink cord, make an overhand knot (see page 31) to anchor the middle of the cord around one end of the cable.

2 Begin making the square knot (see page 27) around the cable. The cable acts as the middle two strands of the square knot, so you are just working with the two outer strands. Continue wrapping the cell cable to the end, and then secure the ends with a barrel knot (see page 26).

3 Thread the neon green cord through the two edge loops closest to one end, and bring the ends round to the front, making sure they are the same length. Criss-cross the contrast cords along the length of the knotted cable.

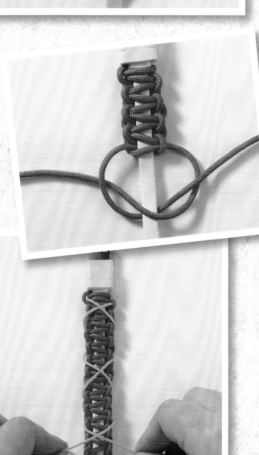

HELPFUL HINTS

To calculate the amount of cord you need, measure the cable and multiply by eight and then cut the pink cord to this measurement. For the green cord, take the cable length, add 4 in. (10 cm) then multiply by two.

If you prefer, you can thread the ends of the contrast cord through the side loops of the square knots at intervals to secure.

PURSE fob

We dress up ourselves, why not dress up our purses and other accessories? Add your favorite pendant to this rosette for an easy-to-make purse fob or keychain.

MATERIALS

Approx. 18 in. (45 cm) of 550 paracord in black

Scissors

Lighter

Fabric glue (optional)

Approx. 8 in. (20 cm) of 550 paracord in black

Decorative bead dangle or hanging pendant

Jump ring

Pliers

1. Using the longer length of cord, make a rosette (see page 34). On the reverse, trim and singe the cord ends (see page 20). If necessary add a dab of glue under each end to stop the rosette from unraveling.

2. Thread the ends of the shorter cord through a loop in the back to form a loop at the top of the rosette. Trim the excess cord ends and singe. Add a small dab of fabric glue to hold the loop in place if needed.

3 Pull a loop of the rosette down at the bottom and attach a dangle of your choice using a jump ring.

HELPFUL HINTS
I've used a purchased dangle, but you could make your own using the instructions on page 22.

chapter 3

FOR THE GUYS

HEX NUT *bracelet*

The 550 paracord and hardware hex nuts combine to create this stylish bracelet with a masculine feel. It uses a variation of the square knot.

1. Attach the cords (see tip box) to the U section of the clasp using a lark's head knot (see page 25). Begin making a half square knot following steps 1–3 on page 27. Repeat this sequence again.

MATERIALS

Approx. 54 in. (135 cm) of 550 paracord in olive drab (grayish green)

Stainless steel U-shackle clasp

10 silver hex nuts

Scissors

Lighter

2. Slide a hex nut onto the two center strands. Create two additional half square knots just as above. Continue this sequence of adding a hex nut followed by two half square knots until you have the length desired.

HELPFUL HINT

Measure the wrist and add 2 in. (5 cm), then mulitply by two—this is the length of the center cord. Multiply the wrist measurement by eight to determine the length of the outer cord.

3. Thread the first outer strand through the clasp from left to right. Thread the second outer strand through the clasp from right to left. Pull the clasp up to the bracelet.

4 Turn the bracelet over and bring all the cords around to the back.

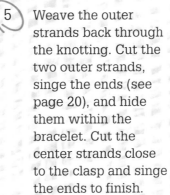

5 Weave the outer strands back through the knotting. Cut the two outer strands, singe the ends (see page 20), and hide them within the bracelet. Cut the center strands close to the clasp and singe the ends to finish.

SHARK'S TOOTH
necklace

When you need a gift for a guy, this is the perfect solution. Any man will love this masculine necklace in camouflage colors with a shark's tooth pendant.

① Find the center of the cords, thread them through the hex nut so it sits in the center and secure with an overhand knot (see page 31).

MATERIALS

Approx. 188 in. (470 cm) of micro paracord in olive green

Approx. 188 in. (470 cm) of micro paracord in tan

Approx. 188 in. (470 cm) of micro paracord in brown

Silver hex nut

Scissors

Lighter

Shark's tooth pendant

② Divide the strands in half. Take one set of strands and create a bight over the other set of strands back towards the beginning of the bracelet. Pass the running ends under the stationary strands and up through the loop.

③ To complete the other half of the knot, create another bight. Pass the running ends under the stationary strands, then back over and through the loop as shown in the picture. This completes the first knot. Repeat these two steps until you have the desired length of necklace.

4 Make a loop at the other end large enough to go over the hex nut toggle and secure with a barrel knot (see page 26). At the center of the necklace tie on the shark's tooth pendant with an overhand knot (see page 31).

HELPFUL HINTS

The hex nut just needs to be large enough to act as a toggle, so you can use any spare one you happen to have in your toolbox.

The cord lengths in the materials list are based on 3 knots measuring 1 in. (2.5 cm) of finished necklace.

TUBE *bracelet*

What I love about this knot is that, unlike many other knots associated with paracord, it creates an attractive tubular pattern with two swirling colors. This royal crown sinnet knot (as shown on page 39) can be used for a great basic tube necklace for interchangeable pendants or to create a bracelet in your favorite team colors.

MATERIALS

Approx. 60 in. (150 cm) of 275 tactical paracord in orange

Approx. 60 in. (150 cm) of 275 tactical paracord in dark blue

Approx. 14 in. (35 cm) of 275 tactical paracord in orange

Approx. 10–12 in. (25–30 cm) of 275 tactical paracord in dark blue

Scissors

Lighter

1   Using the two longer lengths, wind the first color twice around your finger. Slide the second color through both loops on your finger.

2   Take the right side of the second cord, and loop it back over the top, down through the center and under the remaining cord out the other side. Take the left side of the same cord, and loop it back over the top, down through the center and under the remaining cord out the other side.

3   Cinch the knot tight and adjust to create a square form. This is the basic square structure of the royal crown sinnet knot.

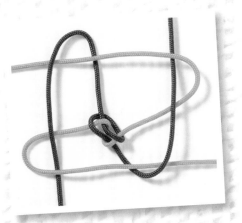

4   Separate the strands so one color runs side to side and the other color up and down, then start to weave the colors around each other as explained on pages 39–41.

5   Continue the pattern to create the length of rounded cord needed for the project. Check your pattern at regular intervals to make sure it is spiraling.

6   Using the short length of orange, make a popcorn ball (see page 32) to fit into the loop at the start. Insert the strand end from the popcorn ball into the tube. Bind everything together with a barrel knot (see page 26) using the short length of dark blue. Cut off any ends and singe (see page 20).

HELPFUL HINTS

Regularly check your pattern to make sure that it is creating a swirl of the two colors. If not, undo the knots back to before the mistake and work again from there.

To create a basic necklace to hold a pendant, simply make a longer strand using slightly thinner cord.

WINGED HEART *necklace*

You don't always have to create intricate knots when using paracord. The multicolor strands combined with metal connectors and findings make it easy to create this masculine necklace.

1 Hold all the longer cords together and thread them through the end rings and across the back of the metal connector.

2 On one side thread the cords in and out of the chain links. Repeat on the other side.

3 Pull the chain down next to the ends of the connector. With one of the shorter black cords begin creating a barrel knot (see page 26). Take the one cord end through the end link of the chain and then pull the knot tight. Repeat on the other side of the connector.

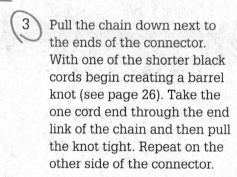

4 Thread a cord end onto one end of the cords and crimp in place. Repeat at the other end and then add a lobster clasp.

MATERIALS

2 approx. 25 in. (62.5 cm) lengths of micro paracord in multicolored black-and-white

2 approx. 25 in. (62.5 cm) lengths of micro paracord in black

Scissors

Lighter

Winged heart metal connector

2 approx. 5 in. (12.5 cm) lengths of chain

2 approx. 10 in. (25 cm) lengths of micro paracord in black

2 cord end crimp beads

Pliers

Lobster clasp

HELPFUL HINT

Singe all the cords together at the ends before you begin. This will make it easier to thread through the chain links and prevent the ends from fraying.

MEN'S *watch*

Make this hunky braided strap to create a chunky watch for the guys. Or try a finer version with thinner cords on a smaller watch for the girls!

MATERIALS

6 approx. 18 in. (45 cm) lengths of 550 paracord in olive drab (grayish green)

Men's watch face with large strap bars

Flat watch clasp with large strap bars

Scissors

Lighter

HELPFUL HINTS

When measuring the wrist to decide on the length of the strap, remember to deduct the length of the clasp and the watch face.

For this project I am making a six-strand braid. You can find the complete instructions in the technique section on page 30.

1. Attach three of the strands to one side of the watch with a lark's head knot (see page 25). Criss-cross the middle two strands, with the left strand over the right.

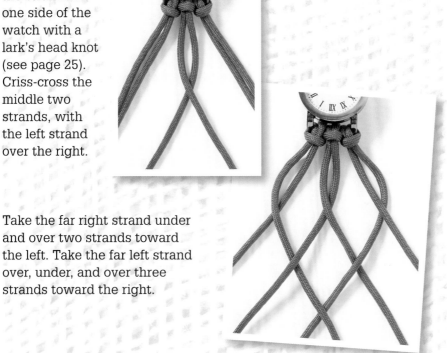

2. Take the far right strand under and over two strands toward the left. Take the far left strand over, under, and over three strands toward the right.

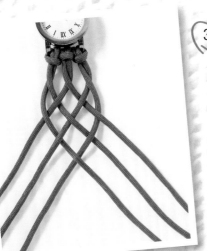

3. Take the far right strand under and over two strands toward the left. Take the far left strand over, under, then over three strands toward the right.

4. Pull your strands tight and adjust so that the tension is even. Repeat from the start of step 2.

5. At the end of one side, fold all the strands through one bar of the clasp. On the back, trim and singe the knots (see page 20), tucking them under an adjacent strand. Make the other side of the strap in the same way.

EARTH *bracelet*

Natural colors and simple wooden beads make this bracelet masculine enough for any guy.

MATERIALS
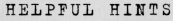

15 in. (37.5 cm) of 275 tactical paracord in green, plus extra for the loop

46 in. (116.5 cm) of micro paracord in beige

6 small beads

Bead reamer (optional)

10 in. (25 cm) of micro paracord in green

Scissors

Lighter

1 larger bead

1. Find the center of the green cord to make a loop. Attach the micro beige cord with an overhand knot (see page 31). With the green cords as the center strands, make four square knots (see page 27) using the beige cords.

2. Take the right beige cord through the center, under and out the left side; take the left beige cord through the center, under and out the right side—this completes one weave. Make about seven weaves in total.

3. Take a small bead. If the hole in the bead is too small for the cords, or doesn't go all the way through the bead properly, use a bead reamer to smooth the inside and make the hole wider.

HELPFUL HINTS
Make the bracelet comfortably snug—paracord has a tendency to stretch.

The exact number of square knots and weaves is not important—start by measuring the wrist, allowing a little extra for fastening and comfort. Divide the measurement to get a length for each section, so the beads will fall in the middle of the bracelet.

4 Thread the left beige running end through the first bead from left to right; then thread the right beige running end from right to left. Pull to tighten. Criss-cross the cords behind the green strands and underneath the bead to secure. Repeat to add the other five beads. Repeat the weaving and square knot sections in steps 2 and 1 in reverse.

5 At the end of the bracelet make a loop with one 275 green strand just large enough to go over the toggle bead. Secure the loop with a barrel knot (see page 26) in the green micro paracord. Trim the other cord away. Singe ends.

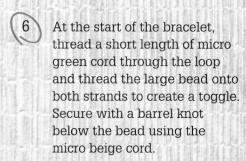

6 At the start of the bracelet, thread a short length of micro green cord through the loop and thread the large bead onto both strands to create a toggle. Secure with a barrel knot below the bead using the micro beige cord.

LONE STAR *keychain*

Keep keys safe but easy to find by hooking the end of this onto on a belt and tucking the keys on the end of the chain into a pants pocket. This variation of the Celtic knot creates a nice decorative bar.

MATERIALS

2 approx. 35 in. (88 cm) lengths of 275 paracord in gray

2 approx. 35 in. (88 cm) lengths of 275 paracord in navy blue

Scissors

Lighter

Heavy-duty metal star snap

Bench block

Rivet setting tool

Hammer

D-ring

Approx. 20 in. (50 cm) of metal chain

2 S-hooks or large jump rings

Swivel trigger clasp

① 1 Hold the gray and blue cords together and find the center. Criss-cross the cords as shown in the photo.

② Take the top right running ends and bring them under the next set of cords to the left. Take the left running ends and bring them over and under the cords to the right.

③ Repeat step 2 until the strap is the length you want. Finish by taking the ends round to the back, weave them through a few knots, keeping to the pattern as much as possible. Trim and singe as explained on page 20.

HELPFUL HINTS

If you don't want to set a snap you could add a D-ring to each end of the strap and hook them together with another trigger clasp.

This variation of the Celtic knot also makes a decorative belt.

④ Press the end of the snap through the cords in the center toward the end of the bar. Place on the bench block rivet side down. Press the snap back onto the reverse.

5. Insert the rivet tool into the center of the snap back. Hammer down firmly. Repeat to add the other half of the snap on the opposite side on the other end of the strap.

6. Add a D-ring onto the strap and snap closed. Add the length of chain using an S-hook or large jump ring. Repeat at the other end of the chain to add the swivel trigger clasp.

CAMOUFLAGE *belt*

This stylish belt is made using a variation of the common square macramé knot and is a great accessory for both guys and gals.

MATERIALS

2 approx. 332 in. (830 cm) lengths of 550 paracord in camouflage

2 approx. 96 in. (240 cm) lengths of 550 paracord in camouflage

Belt buckle

Lacing needle

Scissors

Lighter

1 Attach the cords on each side of the buckle pin with lark's head knots (see page 25), placing the shorter lengths in the center of the left and right groups of strands. Working on the left group of four strands, take the right outer strand over the center strands and under the left.

2 Take the left outer strand under the center strands and up through the loop to complete the first half of the square knot.

3 Repeat this step using the right set of four strands to create a half square knot.

HELPFUL
HINTS

You will need approx 8 in.
(20 cm) of cord for each
1 in. (25 cm) of knotting.

Tape a paper tape
measure to your work
surface so you can quickly
measure the knotting.

To keep track of the cords
during a particular step,
I often number them
from 1 to 6 from the left.

4 Make the second half of the
square knot on the left side
(see steps 4 and 5 of square
knot on page 27). Take the
left-hand strand from the
right-hand group of strands
and thread it through the
square knot on the left.

5 Pull the cords on the left set to
finish the square knot. On the
right hand group of strands,
take the left-hand strand over
the center two strands and
under the right strand.

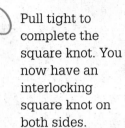

6 Take right strand on the right set of strands under the center and up through the loop.

7 Pull tight to complete the square knot. You now have an interlocking square knot on both sides.

8 Repeat this sequence of steps 1–7 until the belt is the length desired. Create a half square knot using the two sets of outer strands, leaving four strands in the center.

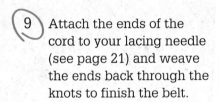

9 Attach the ends of the cord to your lacing needle (see page 21) and weave the ends back through the knots to finish the belt.

10 Cut off the excess cord, leaving about ¼ in. (5 mm). Singe the ends (see page 20) and tuck under the loops on the reverse to finish.

11 To fasten the belt just thread the buckle pin through the center of the belt between knots at a suitable point.

BRADED *lanyard*

Many people need to wear security passes or fobs on a lanyard. Why not create your own personalized version in your favorite colors?

1. To make the strap, first find the centers of the longer gray and dark blue cords. Make a loop in the center of the gray cord and then loop the dark blue around it. Criss-cross the ends of the dark blue cord in the front with the right side cord over the left.

2. Take the right running end around to create a bight, go under all the cords, then back up through the loop and out the top, ending on the right again. Repeat with the left-hand end but to the left. Pull tight.

3. Take the right gray running end and create a bight over the top of the right dark blue cord, through the center, and out the loop on the right.

4. Take the left running end and create a bight over the top of the left dark blue cord. Take the running end up through the center of the right loop, over the top of the loop, and back under the dark blue cord, then out on the left.

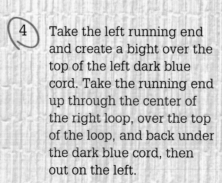

MATERIALS

Approx. 246 in. (615 cm) of 275 paracord in gray

Approx. 92 in. (230 cm) of 275 paracord in dark blue

Metal clip

2 approx. 26 in. (65 cm) lengths of 275 paracord in dark blue

Approx. 10 in. (25 cm) of 275 paracord in orange

Scissors

Lighter

HELPFUL HINTS

I chose this style of knot for the strap because it lies nice and flat against your neck, but you could substitute the square knot (see page 27) or Celtic knot (see page 36) for a different look.

For a more whimsical, fun lanyard, use bright colors together.

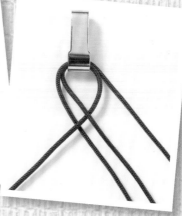

5. Pull the knot up tight and manipulate until it's even. Repeat steps 3–5 to continue making the strap until it is at least 30 in. (75 cm) long. Secure the ends temporarily so they don't unravel as you make the braid.

6. To make the braid, thread the metal clip onto the two remaining dark blue cords up to the center point. Criss-cross the two middle strands with the left over the right. You will have two strands toward the left and two toward the right.

7. Bring the outer left-hand strand under the next strand to the right and then off toward the right. You should now have three strands pointing to the right and one strand to the left.

8. Take the outer right strand, cross it over the next strand to the left and under the following strand. Make sure that your braid resembles that shown in the picture.

9. Take the outer right strand over the next strand to the left, and then take the outer left strand under and over the next two strands to the right. Repeat this sequence until you have the desired length.

10 Thread the ends of the strap through the loop you created at the other end.

11 Thread the ends of the braid through the same loop from bottom to top.

12 Make a barrel knot (see page 26) with orange cord over all of the cords to secure them together. Trim and singe the ends (see page 20).

SPORT *bracelet*

Show team spirit and wear the perfect accessory when working out or playing your favorite sport. In this project, I mix different thicknesses of paracord with a suede leather strap for a trendy look.

MATERIALS

Approx. 20 in. (50 cm) of 275 tactical paracord in black

8 approx. 10 in. (25 cm) lengths of 275 tactical paracord in black

Approx. 24 in. (60 cm) of suede leather cord in gray

Approx. 10 in. (25 cm) of nano paracord in orange

Scissors

Lighter

Approx. 20 in. (50 cm) of nano paracord in black

Large round black bead

HELPFUL HINT

Sometimes the white inner cord shows through when the cord end is sealed, particularly on black cord. If this is the case, touch up with a black permanent marker.

1. Fold over the longer 275 black cord to make a loop in the center and secure just below the loop with a barrel knot (see page 26) using one of the shorter lengths of 275 black cord. Cut the suede cord into three equal lengths, add them to the black cord and secure together with another barrel knot close to the first. Move down about 1 in. (2.5 cm) and secure both black cords and one gray cord with a barrel knot. Pull the ends of the barrel knot slightly but don't tighten all the way.

2. Thread a short length of orange nano cord through the third barrel knot and make a criss-cross on the front. Thread the ends back through the knot and then pull the ends of the barrel knot to tighten completely. Trim the ends of the barrel knot and the orange cord and singe (see page 20).

3. Move down approximately 1 in. (2.5 cm), bring all three grey cords together and add another barrel knot in 275 black cord.

4. Keep repeating steps 1–3 to make knots on alternate strands until the bracelet is the right length. Make a loop at the end with one black cord and secure with a barrel knot. Add a bead toggle as described in step 6 of the Earth Bracelet on page 82.

KNOTTED *cufflinks*

Popcorn balls make ideal cufflinks—make the two balls in team colors for a sport fan, or in gold or silver cord for a more sophisticated look.

MATERIALS

4 approx. 20 in. (50 cm) lengths of 275 paracord in black

4 approx. 20 in. (50 cm) lengths of 275 paracord in orange

2 approx. 10 in. (25 cm) lengths of micro paracord in black

Scissors

Lighter

1. Using the black and orange 275 paracord, make up four popcorn balls (see page 32), two in each color.

2. Taking one ball of each color, overlap the tails.

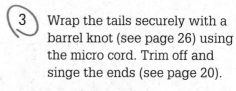

3 Wrap the tails securely with a barrel knot (see page 26) using the micro cord. Trim off and singe the ends (see page 20).

chapter 4

MIXING IT UP

TEARDROP *earrings*

This is a variation of the popcorn knot on page 32. Once you have learnt the basic technique you can then alter it to give you lots of design possibilities.

MATERIALS

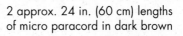

2 approx. 24 in. (60 cm) lengths of micro paracord in dark brown

Scissors

Lighter

2 short lengths of 24-gauge copper wire

Pliers

Pair of earring wires

46 head pins

14 gray beads

16 turquoise beads

16 green translucent beads

1 Make a popcorn ball (see page 32) using one of the lengths of dark brown micro cord. Pull the ends to one side. On the opposite side, pull down three or four loops so they extend out of the bottom of the knot at varying lengths.

2 Push a length of copper wire up through the knot, bending the end so that it catches the knot securely. Wrap the wire around the cord ends and make a loop in the end of the wire. Trim and singe the ends of the cord. Cut off the excess wire and add an earring wire to the loop.

3 Use the head pins and beads to make up beaded dangles as explained on page 22. Add half the dangles to the bottom loops, using the photo as a guide. Repeat all steps for the second earring.

HELPFUL HINT

If you don't want to take the time to make up 46 dangles, use purchased dangles instead.

TRI-STRAND BOHO *bracelet*

So simple to make, this bracelet consists of three different braids. To wear it, simply loop around the wrist a few times and tie in place with the ribbon.

MATERIALS

3 approx. 20 in. (50 cm) lengths of nano paracord in orange

3 approx. 20 in. (50 cm) lengths of micro paracord in brown

20 in. (50 cm) of micro paracord in tan

20 in. (50 cm) of dark turquoise suede cord

20 in. (50 cm) of light turquoise suede cord

Scissors

Lighter

2 large hole European-style rhinestone beads

2 large hole European-style turquoise beads

1 brown bead

6 in. (15 cm) of narrow brown organza ribbon

1. Braids made in different threads can look very different even though they are made with exactly the same technique. The cord at the top is a basic braid in brown micro cord. The middle strand uses the same braiding technique but combines two colors of suede cord with a length of tan micro cord. Orange nano cord was used to create the delicate braid at the bottom. All of the braids use the braiding technique on page 28 with three single strands.

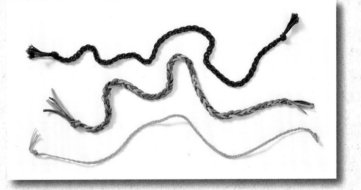

2. Thread the beads onto the orange braid; rhinestone, turquoise, brown, turquoise, rhinestone.

HELPFUL HINTS

You can adjust the bracelet to fit your wrist comfortably by pulling on the ends.

You can make these bracelets in any color you wish or use the colors of your favorite beads.

3. To wear, loop the bracelet around a couple of times and tie the organza ribbon around the overlapping section in a bow.

INDIAN SUMMER
necklace

This necklace shows you how you can combine some of the knots you've already learned in new ways to achieve even more variety.

1. Wrap the washer with some of the orange micro cord to give it a contrasting and decorative touch. Knot the end to the beginning end, trim the excess cord and singe (see page 20).

MATERIALS

Large washer

100 in. (250 cm) of micro paracord in orange

Scissors

Lighter

2 approx. 90 in. (225 cm) lengths of 275 tactical paracord in olive green

2 approx. 100 in. (250 cm) lengths of nano paracord in brown

4 medium bicone wooden beads

20 small round wooden beads

6 dark wooden beads

3 oval wooden beads

2 round beads

2. Thread the ends of the green and the brown cord through the washer until it sits in the middle of the lengths. Grasp the ends together and secure with a barrel knot (see page 26) using some of the orange micro cord. Thread a wooden bicone bead onto both the brown cords.

HELPFUL HINTS
Dark colors usually combine really well, but adding details in a much brighter color will make the design pop.

3. Position the green cords so that they run along the outside of the bicone bead. Secure all strands together after the bicone bead with a barrel knot using some of the orange cord. To add the small beads, tie another short length of brown nano cord onto the green cord below the bicone bead using an overhand knot. Thread a small round wooden bead onto the end of the cord and then take the running end under the green cord to one side of the bicone bead and out at the top.

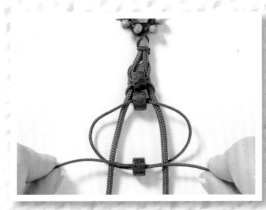

4. Take the running end of the brown cord and thread it up through the loop you just made to anchor the bead. Add 5 beads on each side of the bicone bead in the same way.

5. Criss-cross the brown cord so that the running ends end up below the orange barrel knot. Thread the left running cord through a dark wooden bead and out to the right. Thread the right running cord through the dark bead and out the left. Pull and then criss-cross the ends under the green cords. Repeat to add two more dark beads and then secure this section with another barrel knot in orange cord.

6. Make spaced overhand knots at intervals on each cord, following the photo as a guide. After about 5 in. (12.5 cm), bind all the cords together again with another barrel knot in orange cord. Repeat steps 2–6 on the other side of the washer.

7. Finish the necklace at the back with a loop and bead toggle, using a bicone bead, as explained in steps 5 and 6 of the Earth Bracelet on page 82. Use the remaining beads to make dangles at the front, by knotting them onto short lengths of the green cord, following the photograph.

KNOTTED *necklace*

You don't always have to make complicated knots to make a statement necklace. A simple overhand knot using micro cord and copper rings makes for a delicate yet fashionable necklace.

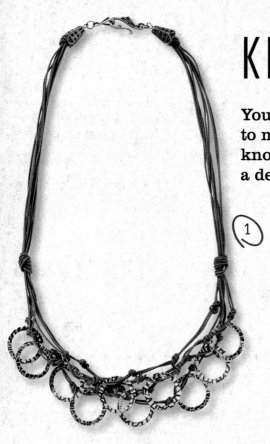

MATERIALS

8 approx. 36 in. (90 cm) lengths of micro paracord in brown

10 metal rings

Scissors

Lighter

2 head pins

2 cone-shaped bead caps

Pliers

1 clasp

1. With the all cords together, tie an overhand knot (see page 31) about 8 in. (20 cm) from one end. Trim and singe the ends (see page 20). Leaving a gap, make an overhand knot using just two strands. Thread one strand over the first ring, through the middle and out the other side. Take the other thread under the first ring, up through the middle and over the other side.

2. Tie the cords together on the other side of the ring with another overhand knot.

3. Add a second ring on two different strands and space it out so it is not bunched up to the first ring. Repeat to add the other 8 rings at intervals. Finish with an overhand knot and trim and singe the ends.

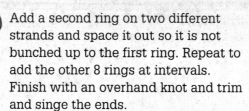

4. Add the cone-shaped bead caps using the head pins as explained in steps 3–5 on pages 46–7. Before closing the loop, add one part of the clasp to each end.

HELPFUL HINTS

For extra decoration you can add bead dangles (see page 22) to the metal rings.

Change the color of the metal rings with a little Rub'n'Buff if necessary.

Every so often I lift the necklace up to see how the loops hang. It is much easier to adjust them as you are going along than if you wait until the design is finished.

HAIR scrunchy

When you make paracord projects, you often end up with lengths of cord that are too short for bracelets, but long enough to keep. Creating hair scrunchies is a great way to use up these extra bits and pieces.

MATERIALS

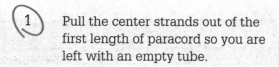

12 in. (30 cm) of 550 paracord in a color of your choice for the band

18 in. (45 cm) of 550 paracord in a contrast color

9 in. (22.5 cm) of elastic stretch cord for jewelry making

Scissors

Lighter

HELPFUL HINT

Be creative when covering the join—sew on a bead or a fabric flower if you don't want to use the popcorns.

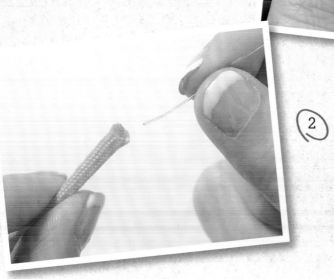

1　Pull the center strands out of the first length of paracord so you are left with an empty tube.

2　Thread the elastic stretch cord through the center of the empty tube and knot the ends. Heat the two ends of the outer tube (see page 20) and push the ends together to seal them while they are still hot. You now have an elasticized scrunchy.

3. Using the contrast color, make up two popcorns (see page 32), working one toward one end of the cord, leaving a gap of around 2 in. (5 cm), and then working the other at the other end of the cord. Trim and singe the outer ends (see page 20) but leave the two popcorns joined. Knot the popcorns over the join in the scrunchy.

TROPICAL PARADISE *earrings*

Mother-of-pearl and turquoise beads give these earrings
a real tropical look but you can vary the colors to match
your outfit if you prefer.

MATERIALS

18 in. (45 cm) of micro paracord
in beige

Scissors

Lighter

8 turquoise square beads

8 head pins

4 jump rings

2 mother-of-pearl feather dangles

Pliers

2 earring wires

HELPFUL HINT

Make another larger version to
create a matching pendant by
using 275 or 425 paracord.

1 Make a rosette
(see page 34) up
to step 6.

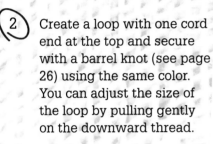

2 Create a loop with one cord
end at the top and secure
with a barrel knot (see page
26) using the same color.
You can adjust the size of
the loop by pulling gently
on the downward thread.

3 Trim and singe all the ends (see page 20). Make up
a dangle with each turquoise bead following the
instructions on page 22. Use a jump ring to attach
four of the dangles and the mother-of-pearl feather
to one of the loops at the bottom of the knot.

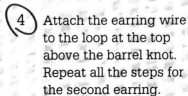

4 Attach the earring wire
to the loop at the top
above the barrel knot.
Repeat all the steps for
the second earring.

TRIBAL DANCE
earrings

So quick and simple to make that you could make a pair to match every outfit. Using a different color of cord and an alternative style of bead can give a completely different look.

(see page 20)

1 Cut a 2 in. (5 cm) length of green cord for the first earring. Singe the ends (see page 20) and while they are still soft, push the two ends together to create a ring.

MATERIALS

4 in. (10 cm) of 550 paracord in green

Scissors

Lighter

Approx. 10 in. (20 cm) of micro paracord in beige

2 flat beads

Approx. 6 in. (15 cm) of micro paracord in green

2 jump rings

Pliers

2 earring wires

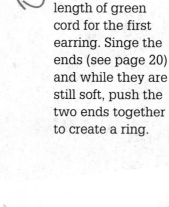

2 Loop a 2 in. (5 cm) length of beige micro cord through the ring and thread a flat bead onto both strands. Secure in place with a barrel knot (see page 26) using green micro cord.

3 Make another barrel knot on the opposite side of the ring using beige micro cord. Thread on a jump ring.

(4) Attach the earring wire onto the jump ring. Repeat the steps to make the second earring.

HELPFUL HINT
I don't like to throw even the smallest of cords away. This is another way to use small bits and pieces and put them to good use.

HEARTS and diamonds

I saw similar bracelets to this in a designer boutique for quite a lot of money. You can design your own in various colors with cup chain, which is flexible rhinestone (diamante) chain. It's easy to bind to cord for a sparkly bracelet.

① Make a barrel knot (see page 26) with the orange cord at one end of the dark brown cord, but don't trim off the running end. Place the cup chain along the top of the cord. Using the running end of the orange cord, wrap around between each rhinestone to secure the cup chain in place. Finish with a barrel knot in orange cord at the other end.

MATERIALS

Approx. 10 in. (25 cm) of 550 paracord in dark brown

Approx. 15 in. (38 cm) of nano cord in orange

Approx. 7½ in. (19 cm) of cup chain

Scissors

E600 silicone-based adhesive

2 cord ends

Heart dangle

Clasp of your choice

Pliers

② Trim the dark brown cord down close to the barrel knots and add a dab of adhesive. Slide on a cord end. Repeat at the other end and leave to dry.

③ Thread on the heart dangle.

④ Add a clasp to the cord ends to finish.

HELPFUL HINTS

You can buy cup chain but you can also recycle it from old jewelry. Look out for broken pieces of jewelry at thrift stores or yard sales, which are inexpensive and a great way to recycle.

To make the bracelet adjustable add a short length of chain to one cord end, which the clasp can hook into at any point.

This bracelet looks great when layered with others, such as the Tri-strand Boho Bracelet on page 102.

LEAF KNOT *earrings*

Simple to make, these are a very effective way to create a chandelier-like design. These eye-catching earrings will draw lots of admiring comments.

MATERIALS

2 approx. 14 in. (35 cm) lengths of 425 paracord in turquoise

Scissors

Lighter

6 metal dangles

8 jump rings

Pliers

2 earring wires

1　Make up a leaf knot (see page 38) using the turquoise cord. Fold the bottom end up and over the front, then through to the back to make a loop at the bottom of the earring. Trim and singe (see page 20).

2　Take the top end over the top and down through the back of the earring, to make a loop at the top of the earring. Trim and singe.

HELPFUL HINT

The dangles used in this project are spinners from a fishing tackle store—look out for interesting bits in stores like this that you can reuse in your projects.

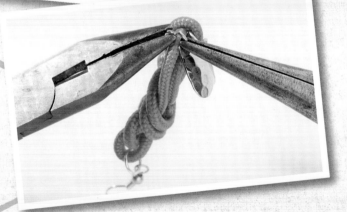

3　Add three dangles to the bottom loop and to the loops at each side using jump rings. Attach an earring wire to the top loop with a jump ring. Repeat all the steps to make the second earring.

CELL PHONE *pouch*

This over-the-shoulder pouch is stylish enough to go out on the town and can be made in an evening. It uses a simple square macramé knot, basket weaving, and braiding.

① Fold the two lengths of cord for the side/bottom strip in half and attach the loops to one of the rings using a lark's head knot, so that two ends of the shorter strand are in the middle. Make square knots (see page 27) until you have enough length to wrap around the sides and bottom of your phone, with the ring protruding at the top. Thread the two center cords over the other silver ring and then down through the center of the knotted strip to secure. Trim the ends close to the knotting and singe (see page 20).

MATERIALS

2 lengths of 550 paracord in camouflage (for measurement see tip box on page 120)

2 silver rings

Scissors

Lighter

Approx. 288 in. (720 cm) of 550 paracord in camouflage

Lacing needle

3 lengths of 550 paracord in camouflage (for measurement see step 11)

E6000 silicone-based adhesive

Cabochon finding (optional)

② Thread the two outer cords down through the center loops to secure. Trim the ends close to the knotting and singe.

③ Take the 288 in. (720 cm) long cord and thread the end into the lacing needle (see page 21).

④ Fold the side/bottom strip made in step 1 into a U shape, with the bottom the width of the phone. Thread the cord through the edge loops on one side of the bottom to secure the end.

HELPFUL HINTS

To estimate how much cord you need for the side/bottom strip of the pouch, measure down the side across the bottom and up the other side of your cell phone and add 4 in. (10 cm). Cut one length of paracord twice this measurement and a second length of paracord eight times this dimension.

Put the cell phone into the pouch after each round of lacing so you can adjust it to fit if necessary.

For extra embellishment, glue a decorative finding on the front of the pouch.

 5 Begin lacing backward and forward across the front of the U shape from the bottom to the top. Don't pull the lacing too tight—keep the sides parallel—or the pouch will end up too small.

6 At the top take the cord over the side and through the loop directly opposite and begin lacing across the other side, working from top to bottom.

7 At the bottom, take the cord through one of the edge loops on the bottom edge and begin weaving in and out of the cross threads from bottom to top and down again.

8 Go through an edge loop each time as you work across the bottom. When you have finished one side, cross over at the top again as in step 6 and weave in and out down the other side.

9 Finish at the bottom corner of the pouch and weave the end through a few loops across the bottom.

10 Cut off the end leaving about ½ in. (1 cm) of cord and singe the end as before. Tuck the end neatly under the next loop.

11 Decide how long you want the strap and cut three strands each twice that length. Fold each cord in half and attach each to the ring with a lark's head knot (see page 25). Using each double cord as one strand, braid the handle as described on page 28. At the final end, fold each pair of cord ends over the second ring and thread the ends back through a few loops on the reverse of the strap.

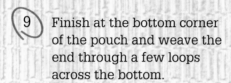

12 Trim off and singe the ends. Add a dab of adhesive under the next loop and then slip the cord end underneath. Glue the finding, if using, to the center front of your pouch.

DOG collars

Both these collars are made using a standard square knot, with either beads or spikes added at intervals. I've also added a bigger decorative bead in the center of the collar for extra bling.

MATERIALS

275 tactical paracord in pink (for measurement see step 1)

275 tactical paracord in orange (for measurement see step 1)

Clasp

2 approx. 10 in. (25 cm) lengths of 275 tactical paracord in pink

Scissors

Lighter

Miscellaneous large hole silver beads or spikes

Large hole crystal bead (optional)

Decorative dangle and jump ring (optional)

Pliers

HELPFUL HINT

Adjust the design by adding or omitting square knots to make the collar the right size for your dog—I have made four square knots between the beads on my pink collar, and added a crystal bead between two silver beads at the center.

1. For a collar around 12 in. (30 cm), cut each cord to approx. 96 in. (240 cm) in length. Find the center of the cord and thread on the clasp. Secure the clasp in place with a barrel knot (see page 26) using the shorter length of pink cord.

2. Begin making the first square knot as explained on page 27 and continue until you have made two complete square knots.

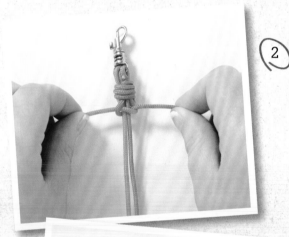

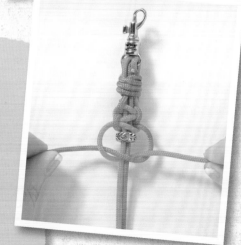

3. Thread a silver bead onto the two center cords. Continue making the next square knot around the bead, anchoring it in place. Repeat the sequence of square knots and beads until the collar is the length you need.

4 At the end thread on the other half of the clasp and make another barrel knot to hold it in place. Trim and singe (see page 20) the ends. Add a decorative dangle—or the dog tag—using a jump ring.

5 The alternative dog collar is made in exactly the same way, using 275 tactical paracord in multi blues and alternating two square knots and a spike. The spike slides between the two center cords, so they sit in the indentation on the spike.

RESOURCES

A helpful list of suppliers for the various tools and materials in this book.

AUTHOR'S WEBSITES

Website:
lindapetersondesigns.com

Facebook:
Linda Molden Peterson

Youtube:
youtube.com/lindapetersondesigns

Pinterest:
lindapetersondesigns

Email:
lindapetersondesigns@yahoo.com

U.S. SUPPLIERS

JEWELRY SUPPLIERS

Beadalon Inc.
www.beadalon.com
Basic jewelry findings, tools,
and small hand tools

Eclectic Products
www.eclecticproducts.com
E6000® silicone-based glue

Fire Mountain Gems
www.firemountaingems.com
Bench block and rivet setting tools

Fiskars
www.fiskars.com
Heavy-duty scissors

I Love to Create
www.ilovetocreate.com
General adhesives, including
Aleene's® Quick Dry Tacky Glue,
OK To Wash-It, Supergel

PARACORD SUPPLIERS

Paracord Galaxy
www.paracordgalaxy.com

Paracord Planet
www.paracordplanet.com

The Paracord Store
www.theparacordstore.com

GENERAL CRAFT STORES
For paracord supplies, jewelry-
making materials, and tools.

A.C. Moore
www.acmoore.com

Hobby Lobby Stores
www.hobbylobby.com

JoAnn Crafts
www.joann.com

Michaels Stores
www.michaels.com

HARDWARE SUPPLIERS
For specialty nuts, bolts,
and chains.

Ace Hardware
www.acehardware.com

Home Depot
www.homedepot.com

Lowe's Inc
www.lowes.com

U.K. SUPPLIERS

JEWELRY SUPPLIERS

The Bead Shop
www.the-beadshop.co.uk
Basic jewelry findings, beads,
charms, bead-making tools

PARACORD SUPPLIERS

**BDU Imports Ltd & The
Bushcraft Store®**
www.thebushcraftstore.co.uk

Wild Elk
www.wildelk.co.uk

GENERAL CRAFT STORES
For paracord supplies, jewelry-
making materials, and tools.

The Craft Barn
www.thecraftbarn.co.uk

Hobbycraft
www.hobbycraft.co.uk

John Lewis
www.johnlewis.com

The Range
www.therange.co.uk

HARDWARE SUPPLIERS
For specialty nuts, bolts,
and chains.

B&Q
www.diy.com

Homebase
www.homebase.co.uk

INDEX

ACKNOWLEDGMENTS

My love and thanks go especially to my husband and best friend of 13 years, Dana—without his help, this book would not have come to be. I am so proud of him, all that he has accomplished, and all that we continue to accomplish together. We make a great team and words do not fully express how much I appreciate his love, patience, and self-sacrifice when it comes to the hours I spend in the studio.

I also could not have possibly accomplished this book without the help of my talented and fantastic team! Even though my name is on the front cover, there are many just as equally important people who are behind the scenes making things happen and they are the absolute best at what they do. A special thanks goes out to my publishers, Cindy Richards and David Peters, along with their talented team of Sally Powell, Carmel Edmonds, and Penny Craig; my personal editor Marie Clayton, who patiently makes sure that my "t"s are crossed and my "i"s are dotted; my photographer Geoff Dann, whose professionalism and photography skills make my work shine brighter than the sun; Marc Harvey who is a tremendous photography assistant; Luis Peral-Aranda for his amazing sense of style when it comes to arranging my work for photography; Emma Mitchell and Gavin Kingcome, the style photographers; and Mark Latter, the book designer.

And certainly, last but not at all least, my daughter Mariah Welsh for lending her youthful hands and being my very patient hand model.

Each one of these people provides a vast amount of knowledge, talent, and experience and I am so grateful to each and every one of you and appreciate the hard work and dedication that you have for your craft and this book. You are the BEST of the BEST!